To: Joan

A dear friend

Love,
Janet
X

DEAR DONNA.
I AM PASSING THIS BOOK OVER
TO YOU; "YOU ARE A GOOD FRIEND"
LOVE ALWAYS
JOAN.

THE NEW YEAR

With time there is no turning back – roll round another year.
The old one with its pangs and pains will find no comrade here.

On towards adventure, facing all the tracks we tread,
To shake hands with the future. Proud to meet what lies ahead.

With time, no turning back. With life, no old regret nor fear.
Start fresh with zest and joy to meet the new unsullied year.

Roses and Japanese anemones

ST VALENTINE'S DAY

The old ways are the sweet ways and the faithful love is best.
The sky love is the deepest love where hearts are happiest.

And so upon St Valentine's the timidest may speak
And ask in the old-fashioned way for that sweet-heart they seek.

With lover's knots and ribboned bows and little frills of lace
That add enchantment to a verse with old-world charm and grace.

Then the maid enjoys the pursuit and the male the fond pursuing. . .
And may the good St Valentine add blessing to the wooing.

MOTHER'S DAY

She is a mother, and how proud her heart
To hear this name upon a child's tongue.
There are rewards for toil and ties and tiredness,
For getting up at night when babes were young.

So often she has seen a pretty garment,
So often she has turned her eyes away
And spent the money on some shoes or trousers
Because the children needed them that day.

But her good care has filled their cheeks with roses,
Has kept them straight of limb and clear of eye.
The truth and pleasant manners that she taught them
May yet repay her as the years go by.

And sometimes when they save their meagre pennies
And buy for her a little bunch of flowers,
She feels as if she is repaid twice over
For all her anxious times and busy hours.

A gift of daffodils

Looking across London, west from the dome of St Paul's

LOOKING AHEAD

May you see beyond the grimy buildings
To all the glory of the highest hill.
May you look beyond the cares of living
To where the promised joy is shining still.

May you see between the narrow roadways
To all the clover growing in the green,
Heeding not the turmoil of existence
Because a blackbird sings above the scene.

Easter chicks

EASTER

Come Easter! with your golden key,
Unlock the winter's mystery.
Such treasures wait upon your will,
Reveal the golden daffodil.
Unlock the tulip's hard green case
And set the jonquil in her place.

For Spring is dancing at your side,
And when the door is open wide,
We shall discover hope anew
Where frosts of grief have changed to dew.

And we shall know in joy sublime
That God was with us all the time,
Guiding us through frost and storm
To Easter days and sunshine warm.

Walking the Mariners' Way near Gidleigh, Devon

PEACEMAKING

Making peace along the byways, in the little lanes of life.
Smooth out the minor matters that are always making strife.

Speak nicely to a stranger and be thoughtful to a friend,
There are many little differences a pleasant word will mend.

In every homely circle there is someone who must be . . .
A peacemaker, a diplomat to help the rest agree.

And even if we cannot spread our wings and travel far,
There's such a lot of quiet work to do just where we are.

So many dismal moods to cheer and sunbeams to release.
The world has room for many more disciples of the peace.

The waterfall at Glenoe, County Antrim

GENEROSITY

Nice to be generous with your car and lift folk here and there,
To fill an empty back seat on an outing anywhere.
But better still to choose the ones without cars of their own,
Who might have spent a sunny Sunday afternoon alone.

It's pleasant to be friendly with the people near at hand,
To include an extra one in little parties that are planned.
But better still to choose the one who hasn't much to do,
Who is rather poor and cannot offer outings back to you.

You're tempted to invite the bright successes much admired,
Who have a crowd of dates, whose company is much desired.
But how much greater to include the lesser known and shy,
To make a point of sharing pleasure with the smaller fry.

A goldfinch and her brood in the ivy

NESTING TIME

Dare to part the rushes beside the waters edge
Peer among the tangle of the honeysuckle hedge.
In the highest treetop or deep down in the corn
Is a hidden nest wherein the baby birds are born.

Marvel at the skill and pattern
Of the perfect plan;
A miracle has taken place
Beyond the skill of Man.

Ellers Wood, Hawnby, North Yorkshire

STARS OF SPRING

Primrose, Star of Spring, a happy heart I'll not deny you.
Welcome here! but I would rather gather you than buy you.

It is my greatest pleasure to go seeking in the dell,
To climb a bank and part the sturdy leaves I love so well.

To hunt in quiet places where a stream will play a tune
And a tiny posy represents a well-spent afternoon.

Here's fragrance for the weary heart by God Himself designed,
Because I gather peace with every primrose that I find.

Bluebell wood

ROBBING THE SPRING

Though not a thief, yet I should like to steal the zest of Spring,
To borrow all her harmony of light and colouring.

To copy in my home the sun and shadows that she blends
And take her joy of living to distribute to my friends.

I'd like no one perfume, but all the fragrance out of doors
To sprinkle in my rooms and wash my cupboards and my floors.

I'd like her calm efficiency about my little toil;
The bravery with which she starts again when projects spoil.

I watch the world with wonder, every cloud and growing thing,
And I try to take a pattern from the wisdom of the spring.

BIRD ON THE WING

He hides upon the spring and sets his song to nature's tune;
He must have passed a hundred views before the day's high noon.
From chimney-pot to crocus bed, from backyard wall to glen;
He knows the haunts of squirrels as he knows the homes of men.

He swoops above the traffic, yet he nestles in the bough
Of almond trees to be in blossom any minute now.
He knows as much of Heaven as he knows about the Earth,
And every resting place rings with his gratitude for birth.

Great tit

WHITSUNTIDE

I looked upon the cherry tree
And all the earth spilled joy for me.
The heavens broke where sunbeams hide
And smiled the smile of Whitsuntide.

The trees, not only green with leaf,
Were blossoming beyond belief.
The fragrance of the morn begun,
Held past and future rolled in one.

Birds sang, grass quivered, flowers swayed.
Spring fairer was because delayed.
I blessed the blossom on the tree
And I beheld eternity.

Magnolia and cherry bloom in Cathedral Close, Norwich

Two friends by the River Forge, North Yorkshire

SMILING ALONG

Roaming the byways outside the great city,
The sky seems too large for my little concerns.
Worries are lost in the green of the landscape,
A sense of wellbeing and wonder returns.

A good wholesome breeze sweeps the frowns
from my forehead.
Here is simplicity, fragrant and free.
It is enough to be living this minute,
To feel and to hear; to think and to see.

My values of living take on a fresh aspect
With every green leaf that I notice unfurled.
Roaming the byways is good as a tonic,
I come home renewed to the work-a-day world.

Snowdrops

WISDOM FROM FLOWERS

The snowdrops have died on the bank by the river,
But as they were fading the crocuses grew.
I remember the scene, bright with yellow and mauve,
When it seemed but a day since the white held the view.

And just as I mourned that the crocus was over,
The tips of the hyacinth broke through the bed,
Followed by others in waxen perfection;
But now there are daffodils dancing instead.

I no longer sigh for the loss of a flower,
But look with expectancy into the grass.
God takes with one hand but gives with another.
Will there be tulips the next time I pass?

Fishing boats at Minehead, Somerset

ST CHRISTOPHER

St Christopher, the kind and strong,
Who helped a little child along
And found he'd saved the world from harm
By lending Christ his valiant arm.

St Christopher, with the Messiah,
Guard the motorist and the flyer;
The big ship and the fisher boat,
The infant with the toy to float.

St Christopher, the traveller's friend,
Protect our journey to the end.
And, by example, make us strong
To help our fellow men along.

Lend us your courage and your smile
To tread in faith the extra mile,
To find our cheerful ways sufficed
To lift the world by helping Christ.

MIDSUMMER DAY

I must hurry, I must hurry, for the early morning light
Has broken through my window, and the roses are in sight.
Green leaves have caught the sunbeams and the dew is on the grass. . .
A petal may have fallen if I linger 'ere I pass.

I must not miss a moment, summer goes too swiftly by;
One day is still the lifetime of a brilliant butterfly.
Fair earth, sweet fragrant summer, full of song and golden rays,
Wait for me to count your treasures, wait for me to add my praise.

The Manor House at Barton, Bedfordshire

Family picnic

THE PICNIC

Maybe the kettle takes longer to boil
And the ground isn't soft as a chair.
Maybe the butter runs soft in the sun
And the cake seems to wilt in the air.

Maybe a wasp drowns himself in the jam
And the leaves float on top of the tea,
And maybe you get a bit cramped in your foot
When you balance a plate on your knee.

But you eat from a table the whole long year round,
Politely, from Jan. to December,
While a meal in the open air loosens your laugh
And is always a joy to remember.

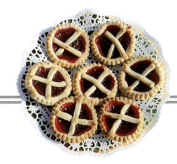

TODAY'S PRAYER

These are the things for which to pray:
Sufficient strength to meet the day;

Sufficient heart to cope with cares
And snags that take us unawares;

Sufficient patience to be found
To keep the peace with those around;

A sense of humour all day long
To turn a sigh into a song;

Sufficient joy of life and health
To live with zest, if lacking wealth;

Eyes that see the inner grace,
The beauty in the commonplace.

Thatching old cottages near Cavendish, Suffolk

Open fire and resident of the Queen's Head Hotel, Icklesham, East Sussex

COMING HOME

In many homes at eventide someone with welcome waits.
Someone lights the fire and sets the knives and forks and plates.

Someone plans a little meal and tidies round the rooms . . .
Maybe fills a vase with oddments from the garden blooms.

Someone waits with little comforts for the ones away,
That home shall be a pleasant sight for those away all day.

So let there be no graceless words, no thankless thoughts and phrases.
When comforts are so customary, we forget the praises.

Let us add a contribution to a home that's dear
And come inside with fond affection, kindness and good cheer.

Seaside sun in Eastbourne, East Sussex

SEA BREEZES AND SUNSHINE

We're happily looking forward to the sea breeze and the rocks,
The summer sun and jolly snapshots in sunbathing frocks.
The high and healthy summits and the song of splashing tides;
The smell of salty seaweed, the picnics and the rides.

We're happy making plans and saving in anticipation,
Painting little pictures of another good vacation.
So that the city views are topped with cliffs of our own making,
And townie flats are filled with the perfume of dreams on waking.

The housewife, shelling peas, is throwing pebbles in the sea,
And the typist writing in the sand with notebook on her knee.

Chrysanthemums

AUTUMN FLOWERS

This is the season of views that are golden,
Of trees that are burnished and leaves edged with gilt.
Sunflowers, dahlias, yellow and shining,
And hedges where splashes of varnish are spilt.

This is the season of red-gold and spun-gold,
Of rosy-gold creeper and coppery fern.
Of wealth in the byways and gleams in the meadow,
Of old-gold and pale-gold wherever we turn.

SHADOWS

We are never surprised when the sun casts a shadow,
In fact we can sit and admire light and shade.
We know that each street has a bright and a dull side,
For that is the way that the world has been made.

Then why be astonished when life casts a shadow,
Obscuring the sun for a moment or two?
This is the way in the course of a lifetime
Of proving the joy and enhancing the view.

A walk in the shade never harms anybody,
It softens hard outlines and brings the heart grace.
Look for the beauty that rests in the shadows
Until the scene shifts and the sun takes its place.

Shadows of Outlaw Crag, looking towards Truss Gap Farm in Swindale, Cumbria

HARVEST FESTIVAL

Although some seeds are wasted and some work destroyed by gale,
Some crops yield unexpectedly, while others seem to fail.
Yet there must be a harvest, the fulfilment of our toil,
The goodness will be gathered after patience from the soil.

And life, too, has a harvest for the aims that we pursue,
Although some good deeds planted do not flourish it is true.
Some plans are disappointing, sown too early or too late,
While impulses of kindness might grow friendships that are great.

Ploughing skill at the Norfolk Shire Horse Centre, West Runton

Tortoiseshell butterflies on Michaelmas daisies

AUTUMN GLORY

What is the glory attached to this season?
Mists in the hedgerows and pearls in the grass!
Why do sweet memories rise without reason
From leaves turning yellow wherever we pass?

Why does the colour of copper and russet
Bring a new warmth to the self-same old earth,
While the ripe fruit weighing down knotted branches
Makes a fresh purpose of song and sweet mirth?

The glory is autumn, as lovely as ever,
Golden with sunshine, but mellow with rain.
Tender with wisdom so quietly gathered,
Autumn, still lovelier, seen once again.

Hollyhocks in a cottage garden in Ashwellthorpe, Norfolk

FLOWERS OF THE FUTURE

These little brown husks in the palm of my hand
Are the flowers of the future that nature has planned.
I can blow them away and they'll fly far and wide,
But a few will take root in the fair countryside.

Here the secrets of life in these fragments remain
To be touched by the magic of sunshine and rain.
What colourful treasures are here in my keeping?
In the palm of my hand summer flowers are sleeping.

Holne Bridge over the River Dart, Devon

BETWEEN SEASONS

Autumn and winter are like old friends meeting,
Who haven't been able to visit before.
They each bring a gift for the love of the other
And wrap it in silver outside the front door.

The gold leaves of autumn are trembling with winter.
The grass by the wayside is spangled with frost.
Old times and old pleasures have now been exchanged
And the new is retold by the leaves twirled and tossed.

Winter and autumn are sharing their memories,
Linked by the sun and the wind – arm in arm.
Soon they will part and fulfil lonely duties,
But together they bring the world beauty and charm.

NOVEMBER SMILES

There'll be heather on the hillside when the mist has rolled away.
There'll be lovely purple patches for the beauty of the day.
November, damp and chilly in tradition of the past,
Shows an ugly countenance that has to smile at last.

And when she smiles there's heather, white and blue and amethyst,
Shining on the hillside with the passing of the mist.
Proving that the world can find an answer to our dreams –
Though trouble comes, it isn't quite as gloomy as it seems.

The lake at Wardour Castle, Wiltshire

Dried flowers

A GARLAND TO REMEMBER

We do not look for primroses in winter,
Nor yearn for blossoms when the trees are bare.
We learn to know the symbols of the seasons
And manage with the blessings that are there.

Nor should we waste our longings on the hopeless,
Nor yearn for things we cannot now afford,
For every circumstance has some advantage,
Just as each season brings its own reward.

Accept life as it comes, now chill, now sunny,
And gather some small garland to remember,
Not seeking holly berries in the summer,
Nor longing for the lilac in November.

AT CHRISTMAS TIME

As time goes by one tends to write less often.
One loses touch with those still dear at heart,
Then Christmas comes with all its great traditions
To bring together those who drift apart.

And every card that bears a scribbled nickname
Revives a story that the past has kept,
And every gift tied with a merry label
Wakens another memory that has slept.

Cats among the presents

A Border collie awaits his duties

TOMORROW WAITS

We never can say at the end of the day:
'My work is accomplished, my duty is done.'
We never can say every hope has been realised,
Each plan is perfected, each aim has been won.

There is always a task or an incident pending,
A few threads of life that are lying untied.
An unfinished duty, some unwritten letters,
A muddle to clear, or a course to decide.

No matter how much has been done and forgotten,
How many decisions and plans have gone through,
There is just as much waiting for us on the morrow
Of problems unsolved and of tasks that are new.

For this is the way that life has to revolve,
There is never a full stop as long as we live.
There is the interest, this is the pleasure . . .
Something to take from life, something to give.

GOOD WISHES

To wish you 'Good Morning', the sun on the lattice,
To give you sweet thought, sing the birds in the trees.
To bring you bright wisdom, the dew on the flowers,
With peace for your vision and joy for your ease.

Perfume at twilight to comfort your dreaming,
Quiet at sundown when shadows descend.
A stream with a melody lapping a lullaby,
Good wishes, Good night and God bless you, my friend.